Love Letters From God

Scriptures and Faith-Builders
That Show God's Love for You

by
Connie Witter

Harrison House
Tulsa, Oklahoma

*Love Letters From God – Scriptures and
Faith-Builders That Show God's Love for You*
ISBN 0-89274-829-X
Copyright © 1995 by Connie Witter
P. O. Box 3064
Broken Arrow, Oklahoma 74013-3064
2nd Printing
Over 20,000 in Print
Published by Harrison House, Inc.
P. O. Box 35035
Tulsa, Oklahoma 74153

Introduction

Love Letters From God is a power-packed combination of confessions and Scripture that will charge you up and inspire you in your daily walk with God.

More than 80 confessions and 150 supporting Scriptures have been included regarding God's thoughts and promises concerning you. As a believer, when you confess God's Word, you agree with what is already true. These confessions and Scriptures put you in remembrance and in line with God's loving thoughts and His many promises toward you as His child.

Love Letters From God is a treasury of reassurance and truth as to how God sees you and what He has promised to you. Read it daily. It will renew your mind with the lovingkindness God has toward you.

"*For I know the plans I have for you,*" *declares the Lord,*
"*plans to prosper you and not to harm you,*
plans to give you hope and a future."
Jeremiah 29:11 NIV

*H*eavenly Father, You have a special purpose and plan for my life. I will trust You to perform on my behalf. For You will bring to pass Your plans for me and You will complete them!

■ ■ ■

I will cry to God Most High, Who performs
on my behalf and rewards me [Who brings to pass
His purposes for me and surely completes them!]
Psalm 57:2 AMP

7.

*L*ord, my confidence is in You. I rest secure
because I know that You are at work on my behalf.
You are fitting everything into a plan for my good
because You have called me according to Your purpose.

◼ ◼ ◼

*W*e are assured and know that [God being a partner
in their labor] all things work together and are
[fitting into a plan] for good to and for those who love
God and are called according to [His] design and purpose.
Romans 8:28 AMP

8.

*M*y life is in Your hands, Lord. I submit my whole
life to You. You created me for a special reason
and You will fulfill Your purpose for me.

■ ■ ■

*T*he Lord will fulfill his purpose for me; your love, O Lord,
endures forever – do not abandon the works of your hands.
Psalm 138:8 NIV

9.

The word of the Lord came to me, saying, "Before I formed you in the womb I knew you, before you were born I set you apart...."
Jeremiah 1:4,5 NIV

10.

*L*ord, You created me in my mother's womb. You watched in secret, as my body was formed. You wrote down Your plan for my life before I took my first breath. Oh, heavenly Father, how I desire to follow the plan that You created for me.

■ ■ ■

*F*or you created my inmost being; you knit me together in my mother's womb. My frame was not hidden from you when I was made in the secret place. When I was woven together in the depths of the earth, your eyes saw my unformed body. All the days ordained for me were written in your book before one of them came to be.

Psalm 139:13, 15, 16 NIV

11.

*L*ord, I am Your workmanship. You created me
in Christ Jesus so that I might do good works.
The work that You have for me to do, You planned
and prepared for me before the creation of the world.

*F*or we are God's [own] handiwork (His workmanship), recreated in
Christ Jesus, [born anew] that we may do those good works which God
predestined (planned beforehand) for us [taking paths which He
prepared ahead of time] that we should walk in them....
Ephesians 2:10 AMP

12.

I give You my worries and my cares, Lord.
For You are always thinking about me and
watching over everything that concerns me.

■ ■ ■

*L*et him have all your worries and cares, for he is always
thinking about you and watching everything that concerns you.
1 Peter 5:7 TLB

13.

*H*ow precious it is, Lord, to realize that you are
thinking about me constantly! I can't even count how many
times a day your thoughts turn towards me. And when
I waken in the morning, you are still thinking of me!
Psalm 139:17,18 TLB

14.

*Y*ou are my heavenly Father and Your thoughts towards me cannot be numbered. How special I must be in Your eyes, Lord, for You to think about me all the time.

■ ■ ■

*M*any, O Lord my God, are the wonderful works which You have done, and Your thoughts towards us; no one can compare with You! If I should declare and speak of them, they are too many to be numbered.

Psalm 40:5 AMP

15.

*L*ord, when I choose to obey Your word, You make me abundantly prosperous in every work of my hands. You take great delight in prospering me. For You are my heavenly Father and it pleases You to see me prosper.

■ ■ ■

*A*nd you shall return and obey the voice of the Lord and do all His commandments which I command you today. And the Lord your God will make you abundantly prosperous in every work of your hand... for the Lord will again delight in prospering you....
Deuteronomy 30:8,9 AMP

16.

*L*ord, absolutely nothing is impossible with You. For no promise that You have spoken in Your Word is without power or impossible of fulfillment in my life.

■ ■ ■

*F*or with God nothing is ever impossible and no word from God shall be without power or impossible of fulfillment.
Luke 1:37 AMP

17.

I am the Lord, the God of all mankind. Is anything too hard for me?
Jeremiah 32:27 NIV

18.

I commit my works into your hands, Lord, for when I trust my life to You, You cause my thoughts to become agreeable with Your will for me. Therefore, Your plans become my plans and they prosper and succeed.

▨ ▨ ▨

*R*oll your works upon the Lord [commit and trust them wholly to Him; He will cause your thoughts to become agreeable to His will, and] so shall your plans be established and succeed.
Proverbs 16:3 AMP

19.

*L*ord, You did not create me to be a failure.
You created me to be a success. For You have promised
that if I will meditate on Your Word and walk in Your ways,
my life shall be prosperous and successful.

■ ■ ■

*D*o not let this Book of the Law depart from your mouth;
meditate on it day and night, so that you may be careful to do
everything written in it. Then you will be prosperous and successful.
Joshua 1:8 NIV

20.

$\mathcal{L}$ord, I am confident in You. I rest in the promises that You have given me. For in every situation I remember that You said, all things are possible to those who believe.

■ ■ ■

•••$\mathcal{A}$*ll things are possible to him who believes.*
Mark 9:23 NAS

21.

My son, if your heart is wise, then my heart will be glad;
my inmost being will rejoice when your lips speak what is right.
Proverbs 23:15,16 NIV

22.

*L*ord, You love me with an everlasting love.
Your love for me will never fail. You are my heavenly
Father and You will never stop loving me.

*T*he Lord appeared...saying: *"I have loved you with an everlasting
love; I have drawn you with loving-kindness."*
Jeremiah 31:3 NIV

23.

*H*eavenly Father, how wonderful it is to know
that you want the best for me. For you have shown me
through your Word that you wish above all things that
I would prosper and be in health, even as my soul prospers.

*B*eloved, I wish above all things that thou mayest
prosper and be in health, even as thy soul prospereth.
3 John 2

24.

*Y*ou are my heavenly Father and nothing is beyond Your ability. For You are able to carry out Your purpose for me and do exceedingly above my highest thoughts, hopes, or dreams.

*N*ow to Him Who...is able to [carry out His purpose
and] do superabundantly, far over and above all that we
[dare] ask or think [infinitely beyond our highest prayers,
desires, thoughts, hopes, or dreams].
Ephesians 3:20 AMP

Do not let your hearts be troubled [distressed, agitated]. You believe in and adhere to and trust in and rely on God...and trust in and rely also on Me (Jesus). Peace I leave with you; My [own] peace I now give and bequeath to you. Not as the world gives do I give to you. Do not let your hearts be troubled, neither let them be afraid. [Stop allowing yourselves to be agitated and disturbed; and do not permit yourselves to be fearful and intimidated and cowardly and unsettled.]
John 14:1,27 AMP

26.

*H*eavenly Father, what an incredible quality of love
You have shown towards me, that You would allow me
to be called and counted as Your child.

■ ■ ■

*S*ee what [an incredible] quality of love the Father has given
(shown, bestowed on) us, that we should [be permitted to] be
named and called and counted the children of God!
1 John 3:1a AMP

27.

May the words of my mouth and the meditation of my heart be pleasing in your sight, O Lord, my Rock and my Redeemer.
Psalm 19:14 NIV

28.

*H*eavenly Father, I put my hope in Your unfailing love, for You have promised that I shall never be disappointed when I put my hope in You.

*T*he Lord delights in those who fear him,
who put their hope in his unfailing love.
Psalm 147:11 NIV

*T*hen you will know that I am the Lord; those who
hope in me will not be disappointed.
Isaiah 49:23c NIV

29.

*H*eavenly Father,
I faint for your salvation; but I expect your help, for you have promised it. My eyes are straining to see your promises come true. You are my refuge and my shield, and your promises are my only source of hope.
Psalm 119:81,82a,114 TLB

30.

*L*ord, I will not worry about anything; instead I will take all my concerns to You in prayer. When I give You my cares, You give me Your peace. Your peace keeps my thoughts at rest when I put my trust in You.

■ ■ ■

*D*on't worry about anything; instead, pray about everything; tell God your needs and don't forget to thank him for his answers. If you do this you will experience God's peace, which is far more wonderful than the human mind can understand. His peace will keep your thoughts and your hearts quiet and at rest as you trust in Christ Jesus.

Philippians 4:6,7 TLB

31.

$\mathcal{W}$*e wait in hope for the Lord; he is our help and our shield. In him our hearts rejoice, for we trust in his holy name. May your unfailing love rest upon us, O Lord, even as we put our hope in you.*
Psalm 33:20-22 NIV

32.

*Y*ou will guard me and keep me in perfect peace when I keep my mind on You. I commit myself to You, Lord, I lean on You and hope confidently in what You have promised me. For You are my everlasting strength.

■ ■ ■

*Y*ou will guard him and keep him in perfect and constant peace whose mind...is stayed on You, because he commits himself to You, leans on You and hopes confidently in You. So trust in the Lord (commit yourself to Him, lean on Him, hope confidently in Him) forever; for the Lord God is an everlasting Rock....

Isaiah 26:3,4 AMP

33.

Thus says the Lord...I will pour My Spirit upon your offspring, and My blessing upon your descendants. And they shall spring up among the grass like willows or poplars by the watercourses. One shall say, I am the Lord's...another will write [even brand or tattoo] upon his hand, I am the Lord's....

Isaiah 44:2-5 AMP

34.

I am never alone, for You are always with me.
You are my heavenly Father and You will always be
there to help me in my time of need.

*G*od is our refuge and strength, an ever-present help in trouble.
Psalm 46:1 NIV

35.

*F*or I am the Lord, your God, who takes hold of your right hand
and says to you, Do not fear; I will help you.
Isaiah 41:13 NIV

36.

*L*ord, I put my confidence in You concerning my children.
Your Word says that when I train them to follow Your ways,
when they are old they will not depart from them.
For You have promised that Your righteousness shall
be with my children and my children's children.

◼ ◼ ◼

*T*rain a child in the way he should go,
and when he is old he will not turn from it.
Proverbs 22:6 NIV

*B*ut from everlasting to everlasting the Lord's love is with those
who fear him, and his righteousness with their children's children.
Psalm 103:17 NIV

37.

"As for me, this is my covenant with them," says the Lord. "My Spirit, who is on you, and my words that I have put in your mouth will not depart from your mouth, or from the mouths of your children, or from the mouths of their descendants from this time on and forever," says the Lord.
Isaiah 59:21 NIV

38.

*L*ord, I trust in Your Word. For You have said that my
children shall be disciples of the Lord, taught by You
and obedient to Your will; and great shall be the
peace and undisturbed composure of my children.

*A*nd all your [spiritual] children shall be disciples [taught by the
Lord and obedient to His will], and great shall be the peace and
undisturbed composure of your children.
Isaiah 54:13 AMP

39.

Now therefore listen to me, O you sons; for blessed (happy, fortunate, to be envied) are those who keep my ways.

Proverbs 8:32 AMP

40.

*F*ollowing after you, Lord, is profitable in every way. For You have not only promised me eternal life in heaven, but You have also promised me abundant life on earth.

■ ■ ■

...*g*odliness (spiritual training) is useful and of value
in everything and in every way, for it holds promise for the
present life and also for the life which is to come.
1 Timothy 4:8 AMP

41.

O my God, I trust, lean on, rely on and am confident in You. Let me not be put to shame or [my hope in You] be disappointed...for You are the God of my salvation....
Psalm 25:2,5 AMP

I put my confidence in You, Lord, for You will never fail me.
Therefore, I trust in Your promises. For You are my
heavenly Father and You have said I will not be
disappointed when I put my trust in You.

*...b*ut he who believes in Him [who adheres to,
trusts in, and relies on Him] shall not be put to shame
nor be disappointed in his expectations.
Romans 9:33 AMP

43.

*...I have created you and cared for you since you were born.
I will be your God through all your lifetime, yes, even when
your hair is white with age. I made you and I will care for you.
I will carry you along and be your Savior.
Isaiah 46:3,4 TLB*

44.

I will boldly speak of Your promises, Lord,
for I know Your Word is true. For I will never be
put to shame, when I put my hope in You.

*N*o one whose hope is in you will ever be put to shame....
Psalm 25:3 NIV

45.

...You are precious to me and honored, and I love you.
All who claim me as their God will come, for I have made
them for my glory; I created them.
Isaiah 43:4,7 TLB

46.

I will not worry about my needs, Lord. For You are my heavenly Father and You have promised to take care of me. I will seek You first and all that I need You will provide.

*T*herefore I tell you, do not worry about your life, what you will eat or drink; or about your body, what you will wear.... Look at the birds of the air; they do not sow or reap or store away in barns, and yet your heavenly Father feeds them. Are you not much more valuable than they? Who of you by worrying can add a single hour to his life? So do not worry, saying, "What shall we eat?" or "What shall we drink?" or "What shall we wear?" For the pagans run after all these things, and your heavenly Father knows that you need them. But seek first his kingdom and his righteousness, and all these things will be given to you as well.

Matthew 6:25-27,31-33 NIV

47.

O Lord, You have examined my heart and know everything about me. You know when I sit or stand. When far away you know my every thought. You chart the path ahead of me, and tell me where to stop and rest. Every moment, you know where I am. You know what I am going to say before I even say it. You both precede and follow me, and place your hand of blessing on my head.

Psalm 139:1-5 TLB

48.

*L*ord, You are Jehovah Jireh, my Provider. For You will supply
all of my needs according to Your riches in Christ Jesus.

*A*nd my God will meet all your needs according
to his glorious riches in Christ Jesus.
Philippians 4:19 NIV

49.

*H*eavenly Father,
Though I walk in the midst of trouble, you preserve my life;
you stretch out your hand against the anger of my foes,
with your right hand you save me.
Psalm 138:7 NIV

50.

*L*ord, nothing I do goes without Your notice. You take great interest in every aspect of my life. You know me so intimately that the very hairs of my head You have numbered.

*A*re not two little sparrows sold for a penny? And yet not one of them will fall to the ground without your Father's leave (consent) and notice. But even the very hairs of your head are all numbered. Fear not, then; you are of more value than many sparrows.

Matthew 10:29-31 AMP

51.

I call on you, O God, for you will answer me; give ear to me
and hear my prayer. Show the wonder of your great love, you who
save by your right hand those who take refuge in you.... Keep me
as the apple of your eye; hide me in the shadow of your wings.

Psalm 17:6-8 NIV

52.

*L*ord, You are my Shepherd, You guide and lead me, and I listen to Your voice. You call me by name and instruct me in the way I should go. I follow You, Lord, because I know Your voice and the voice of a stranger I will not follow.

■ ■ ■

*B*ut he that entereth in by the door is the shepherd of the sheep...the sheep hear his voice: and he calleth his own sheep by name, and leadeth them...and the sheep follow him: for they know his voice. And a stranger will they not follow....

John 10:2-5

*I [the Lord] will instruct you and teach you in the way you should go;
I will counsel you with My eye upon you. And your ears will hear
a word behind you, saying, This is the way; walk in it, when you
turn to the right hand and when you turn to the left.*
Psalm 32:8 AMP; Isaiah 30:21 AMP

54.

*H*eavenly Father, Your love for me is unconditional.
For nothing I have done in the past or would ever do
in the future could ever separate me from Your great
love which is in Christ Jesus my Lord.

*F*or I am convinced that neither death nor life, neither angels nor
demons, neither the present nor the future, nor any powers, neither
height nor depth, nor anything else in all creation, will be able to
separate us from the love of God that is in Christ Jesus our Lord.
Romans 8:38,39 NIV

55.

*Fear not [there is nothing to fear], for I am with you;
do not look around you in terror and be dismayed,
for I am your God. I will strengthen and harden you to difficulties,
yes, I will help you; yes, I will hold you up and retain you
with My [victorious] right hand of rightness and justice.
Isaiah 41:10 AMP*

56.

*O*h, heavenly Father, how much you must love me,
to send Your Son to die in my place. For He was wounded
for my transgressions. He was bruised for my iniquities.
He took the punishment that brought me peace
and prosperity and by His stripes I am healed.

*B*ut He was wounded for our transgressions, He was bruised
for our guilt and iniquities; the chastisement [needful to obtain]
peace and well-being for us was upon Him, and with the stripes
[that wounded] Him we are healed and made whole.

Isaiah 53:5 AMP

57.

*ℒead me, O Lord, in your righteousness...make straight
your way before me. Show me your ways, O Lord, teach me
your paths; guide me in your truth and teach me, for you are
God my Savior, and my hope is in you all day long.*
Psalm 5:8; 25:4,5 NIV

58.

$\mathcal{L}$ord, I pray that I would be rooted and grounded in Your love, that I might have the power to understand how wide and long and high and deep Your love is for me. I pray that I would know Your love that surpasses knowledge, so that I might be filled with the fullness of God.

...$\mathcal{I}$ pray that you, being rooted and established in love, may have power, together with all saints, to grasp how wide and long and high and deep is the love of Christ, and to know this love that surpasses knowledge –that you may be filled to the measure of all the fullness of God.

Ephesians 3:17-19 NIV

59.

Now what I am commanding you today is not too difficult for you or beyond your reach. No, the word is very near you; it is in your mouth and in your heart so you may obey it. See, I set before you today life and prosperity, death and destruction. For I command you today to love the Lord your God, to walk in his ways, and to keep his commands... I have set before you life and death, blessings and curses. Now choose life, so that you and your children may live.

Deuteronomy 30:11,14-16,19 NIV

60.

*H*eavenly Father, no matter what problem I may face I know that You will help me, therefore, I will not be ashamed or confused. I am confident because I know I will not be disappointed when I put my trust in you.

■ ■ ■

*F*or the Lord God helps Me; therefore have I not been ashamed or confounded; therefore have I set My face like a flint, and I know that I shall not be put to shame.

Isaiah 50:7 AMP

*Listen, my son, accept what I say, and the years of your life
will be many. I guide you in the way of wisdom and lead you
along straight paths. When you walk, your steps will not
be hampered; when you run, you will not stumble.*
Proverbs 4:10-12 NIV

62.

*H*eavenly Father, sanctify me by separating me from profane
things and make me pure and holy and consecrated to You.
Faithful are You, Who has called me. You are utterly trustworthy
and You will fulfill Your call by keeping me.

■ ■ ■

*And may the God of peace Himself sanctify you...[separate you
from profane things, make you pure and wholly consecrated to God];
and may your spirit and soul and body be...found blameless at the
coming of our Lord Jesus Christ (the Messiah). Faithful is He Who is
calling you [to Himself] and utterly trustworthy, and He will also do it....*
1 Thessalonians 5:23,24 AMP

63.

Heavenly Father,
Remove from me the way of falsehood and unfaithfulness [to You],
and graciously impart Your law to me. I have chosen the way
of truth and faithfulness; Your ordinances have I set before me.
I will [not merely walk, but] run the way of Your commandments,
when You give me a heart that is willing.
Psalm 119:29,30,32 AMP

64.

*H*eavenly Father, You chose me before the creation of the world to be holy and blameless in Your sight. Because of Your great love for me, You adopted me as Your child.

*F*or he chose us in him before the creation of the world to be holy and blameless in his sight. In love he predestined us to be adopted as his sons through Jesus Christ....
Ephesians 1:4,5 NIV

65.

...*O Lord; teach me your decrees. I rejoice in following your statutes as one rejoices in great riches. I meditate on your precepts and consider your ways. I delight in your decrees; I will not neglect your word.*
Psalm 119:12,14-16 NIV

66.

$\mathcal{L}$ord, I am convinced that You will continue to perfect
and develop the good work that You began in me. For as
I trust in You, Your grace is at work in me making me
into everything You created me to be.

■ ■ ■

*$\mathcal{A}$nd I am convinced and sure of this very thing, that He Who
began a good work in you will continue until the day of Jesus Christ
[right up to the time of His return], developing [that good work] and
perfecting and bringing it to full completion in you.*
Philippians 1:6 AMP

67.

...*I will be their God: I will give them singleness
of heart and action, so that they will always fear me for their own
good and the good of their children after them. I will make
an everlasting covenant with them: I will never stop doing good
to them, and I will inspire them to fear me, so that they will never
turn away from me. I will rejoice in doing them good and...
I will give them all the prosperity I have promised them.
Jeremiah 32:38-42 NIV*

68.

I will not weaken in faith, Lord, I will not waver through unbelief concerning Your promises. I will follow the example of my father Abraham and become fully persuaded that You will do exactly what You have promised.

*N*o unbelief or distrust made him waver (doubtingly question) concerning the promises of God, but he grew strong and was empowered by faith as he gave praise and glory to God, fully satisfied and assured that God was able and mighty to keep His word and to do what He had promised.

Romans 4:20,21 AMP

69.

*J*eavenly Father,
Oh, that my ways were directed and established to observe
Your statues [hearing, receiving, loving, and obeying them]!
Then shall I not be put to shame [by failing to inherit
Your promises] when I have respect to all Your commandments.
Psalm 119:5,6 AMP

70.

$\mathcal{L}$ord, I trust You with all my heart, therefore, I will feed upon Your faithfulness. For I will be a living testimony that You are trustworthy and faithful to Your promises. You are my Rock, and there is no unrighteousness in You.

*T*rust (lean on, rely on, and be confident) in the Lord and do good; so shall you dwell in the land and feed surely on His faithfulness....
Psalm 37:3 AMP

[*T*hey are living memorials] to show that the Lord is upright and faithful to His promises; He is my Rock, and there is no unrighteousness in Him.
Psalm 92:15 AMP

71.

*H*eavenly Father,
My eyes fail, watching for Your salvation and for the fulfillment of
Your righteous promise. My life dissolves and weeps itself away for
heaviness; raise me up and strengthen me according to [the promises
of] Your word. Forsake me not, O Lord; O my God, be not far from me.
Psalm 119:123,28; 38:21 AMP

*H*eavenly Father, I trust in Your Word because
what You have said, You will do. For the promises of Your
Word are backed by all the honor of Your name.

...for your promises are backed by all the honor of your name.
Psalm 138:2 TLB

73.

*I will sanctify my great name...and the heathen shall
know that I am the Lord, saith the Lord God, when I shall
be sanctified in you before their eyes.*
Ezekiel 36:23

74.

$\mathcal{L}$ord, I will not forget the benefits of being Your child.
For You have promised to forgive all my sins and
to heal all of my diseases.

$\mathcal{P}$*raise the Lord, O my soul, and forget not all his benefits –*
who forgives all your sins and heals all your diseases.
Psalm 103:2,3 NIV

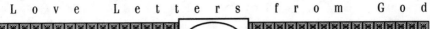

75.

My Son, do not forget my teaching, but keep my commands in your heart, for they will prolong your life many years and bring you prosperity.

Proverbs 3:1,2 NIV

76.

*L*ord, You have said in Your Word that You not only
forgive my sins but You completely forget them. Therefore,
I am free to let go of past mistakes and I will press
towards becoming more like Jesus.

...*f*orgetting what lies behind and reaching forward
to what lies ahead, I press on toward the goal for the prize
of the upward call of God in Christ Jesus.
Philippians 3:13, 14 NAS

77.

*S*earch me, O God, and know my heart;
Try me and know my anxious thoughts;
And see if there be any hurtful way in me,
And lead me in the everlasting way.
Psalm 139:23,24 NAS

*H*eavenly Father, You have made me a new creature in Christ Jesus. My old sins, old mistakes, and old attitudes have passed away, and I have begun a new life of victory.

*T*herefore if any man be in Christ, he is a new creature: old things are passed away; behold, all things are become new.
2 Corinthians 5:17

79.

I, even I, am He Who blots out and cancels your transgressions for My own sake, and I will not remember your sins.
Isaiah 43:25 AMP

I confess my sins before You, Lord. For You are faithful
and just and will forgive my sins and cleanse me
from all unrighteousness.

If we confess our sins, he is faithful and just and will forgive
us our sins and purify us from all unrighteousness.
1 John 1:9 NIV

81.

*Have mercy on me, O God, according to your unfailing love;
according to your great compassion blot out my transgressions.
Wash away all my iniquity and cleanse me from my sin.*

Psalm 51:1,2 NIV

82.

I am Your child, Lord, and You would never lie
to me. Therefore, I trust in Your promises. For what
You have promised in Your Word, You will perform in my life.

■ ■ ■

*G*od is not a man, that he should lie, nor a son of man,
that he should change his mind. Does he speak and
then not act? Does he promise and not fulfill?
Numbers 23:19 NIV

*T*he Lord is faithful to all his promises....
Psalm 145:13b NIV

83.

For I am the Lord; I will speak, and the word that
I shall speak shall be performed (come to pass); it shall be
no more delayed or prolonged...I will speak the word and
will perform it, says the Lord God.

Ezekiel 12:25 AMP

*L*ord, I trust You with all my heart. I will not lean to my own understanding. I will acknowledge You in every decision that I make and You will lead me down the right path.

*T*rust in the Lord with all thine heart; and lean not unto thine own understanding. In all thy ways acknowledge him, and he shall direct thy paths.
Proverbs 3:5,6

85.

*M*y son, pay attention to what I say; listen closely to my words.
*Do not let them out of your sight, keep them within your heart; for they
are life to those who find them and health to a man's whole body.*
Proverbs 4:20-22 NIV

■ ■ ■

86.

*L*ord, I may make many plans but it is Your purpose
for me that will stand. For my steps are ordered by you,
Lord, and you busy yourself with my every step.

*M*any plans are in a man's mind, but it is the Lord's
purpose for him that will stand.
Proverbs 19:21 AMP

*T*he steps of a [good] man are directed and established
by the Lord when He delights in his way [and He busies
Himself with his every step].
Psalm 37:23 AMP

87.

*This is what the Lord says – your Redeemer, the Holy One
of Israel: "I am the Lord your God, who teaches you what is
best for you, who directs you in the way you should go."*
Isaiah 48:17 NIV

88.

*L*ord, I will not become discouraged when a door shuts before me, for You must have something much more wonderful in store for me. For when You open a door, no man will shut it.

... *T*hese are the words of the Holy One, the True One,
He Who has the key of David, Who opens and no one shall shut,
Who shuts and no one shall open: I know your [record of] works
and what you are doing. See! I have set before you a door
wide open which no one is able to shut....
Revelations 3:7,8 AMP

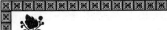

89.

*H*eavenly Father,

Oh, how I love Your law! It is my meditation all the day. Your word is
a lamp to my feet and a light to my path. Your testimonies have I
taken as a heritage forever, for they are the rejoicing of my heart.
Psalm 119:97,105,111 AMP

90.

*H*eavenly Father, You are my refuge, my hightower,
my stronghold in times of trouble. I lean on and confidently
put my trust in You. For You will never fail to help me
when I seek You on the authority of Your Word.

*T*he Lord also will be a refuge and a high tower for the
oppressed, a refuge and a stronghold in times of trouble...
And they who know Your name...will lean on and confidently
put their trust in You, for You, Lord, have not forsaken those who
seek (inquire of and for) You [on the authority of God's Word...].
Psalm 9:9,10 AMP

91.

B̶ut now the Lord who created you...says, Don't be afraid, for I have ransomed you; I have called you by name; you are mine. When you go through deep waters and great trouble, I will be with you. When you go through rivers of difficulty, you will not drown! When you walk through the fire of oppression, you will not be burned up – the flames will not consume you. For I am the Lord your God, your Savior....

Isaiah 43:1-3 TLB

■ ■ ■

92.

*L*ord, You require of me to reverently fear You: that means to walk in Your ways, to love You, and to serve You with all my heart and with my entire being. You want me to obey Your Word so that my life might be filled with Your blessings. Oh, how I desire to please You, Lord, help me to walk in Your ways.

■ ■ ■

*...W*hat does the Lord your God require of you but [reverently] to fear the Lord your God, [that is] to walk in all His ways and to love Him, and to serve the Lord your God with all your [mind and] heart...To keep the commandments of the Lord...for your good.
Deuteronomy 10:12,13 AMP

93.

*H*eavenly Father,
I seek you with all my heart; do not let me stray from
your commands....give me discernment that I may understand
your statues. May my cry come before you, O Lord;
give me understanding according to your word.
Psalm 119:10,125,169 NIV

94.

*I*n my own strength, Lord, I am unable to please You. But as I depend on Your grace, You will create in me the power and desire to do those things that are pleasing in Your sight.

■ ■ ■

*[N*ot in your own strength] for it is God Who is all the while effectually at work in you [energizing and creating in you the power and desire], both to will and to work for His good pleasure and satisfaction and delight.*

Philippians 2:13 AMP

95.

I will bind you to me forever with chains of righteousness and justice and love and mercy. I will betroth you to me in faithfulness and love, and you will really know me then as you never have before.
Hosea 2:19,20 TLB

96.

*H*eavenly Father, I will not become slothful and disinterested in Your Word. I will follow the example of my father Abraham and put my trust in your promises. I will wait patiently for You to perform Your Word in my life.

That ye be not slothful, but followers of them who through faith and patience inherit the promises.
Hebrews 6:12

97.

...Listen to and obey My voice, and I will be your God and you will be My people; and walk in the whole way that I command you, that it may be well with you.

Jeremiah 7:23 AMP

98.

$\mathcal{L}$ord, when I face trouble in my life, I am encouraged by Your promise. For Your Word says, that I may face many problems but You will deliver me out of them all.

$\mathcal{A}$ righteous man may have many troubles, but the Lord delivers him from them all.
Psalm 34:19 NIV

99.

...for He [God] Himself has said, I will not in any way fail you nor give you up nor leave you without support. [I will] not, [I will] not, [I will] not in any degree leave you helpless, nor forsake you nor let you down, (relax My hold on you)! [Assuredly not!]
Hebrews 13:5 AMP

100.

*B*ecause I love You, Lord, You will rescue me;
You will protect me, for I trust in Your name. When I call,
You will answer. You will be with me in trouble, You will
deliver me and honor me. With long life will You
satisfy me and show me Your salvation.

*"B*ecause he loves me," says the Lord, "I will rescue him; I will
protect him, for he acknowledges my name. He will call upon me, and I
will answer him; I will be with him in trouble, I will deliver him and
honor him. With long life will I satisfy him and show him my salvation."*
Psalm 91:14-16 NIV

*...My grace (My favor and loving-kindness
and kindness and mercy), is enough for you, [sufficient against any
danger and enables you to bear the trouble manfully];
for My strength and power are made perfect (fulfilled and
completed) and show themselves most effective in [your] weakness.*
2 Corinthians 12:9a AMP

102.

*L*ord, I will arise from the depression and despair in which
my circumstances have kept me. I will rise to a new life of
victory and I will shine with Your glory as I put my trust in You.

*A*rise [from the depression and prostration in
which circumstances have kept you – rise to a new life]!
Shine (be radiant with the glory of the Lord)....
Isaiah 60:1 AMP

103.

...$\mathcal{D}$o not be seized with alarm and struck with fear; only keep on believing.
Mark 5:36 AMP

104.

*L*ord, never forget the promises that You have given to me,
for they are my only source of hope. They give me strength
in all my troubles; how they refresh and revive me!

■ ■ ■

*N*ever forget your promises to me your servant,
for they are my only hope. They give me strength in
all my troubles; how they refresh and revive me!
Psalm 119:49,50 TLB

105.

*H*eavenly Father,
The law from your mouth is more precious to me than
thousands of pieces of silver and gold. I rejoice in your
promise like one who finds great spoil. You are my refuge
and my shield; I have put my hope in your word.
Psalm 119:72, 162, 114 NIV

106.

$\mathcal{L}$ord, I put You in remembrance of Your promises. I will not keep silent. I will speak of them in the morning and I will speak of them at night. For I am confident that you are faithful to Your Word and You will do what You have promised.

...$\mathcal{Y}$ou who [are His servants and by your prayers] put the Lord in remembrance [of His promises], keep not silence.
Isaiah 62:6 AMP

...$f$or He Who promised is reliable (sure) and faithful to His word.
Hebrews 10:23 AMP

107.

For I will restore health to you, and I will heal your wounds, says the Lord....
Jeremiah 30:17 AMP

...for I am the Lord, Who heals you.
Exodus 15:26 NIV

108.

*L*ord, no one has heard, nor perceived with the ear, nor has eye seen a God besides You. For You work strong and show Yourself active on my behalf when I earnestly wait for You.

■ ■ ■

*F*or from of old no one has heard nor perceived by the ear, *nor has the eye seen a God besides You, Who works and shows Himself active on behalf of him who [earnestly] waits for Him. Isaiah 64:4 AMP*

109.

I am with you and will watch over you wherever you go....
I will not leave you until I have done what I have promised you.
Genesis 28:15 NIV

110.

I put my trust in You, Lord, therefore I rejoice. I sing and shout for joy because You make a covering over me and protect me. I am joyful in You, Lord, for You place Your hand of blessing upon my life and surround me with Your favor as a shield.

But let all who take refuge in you be glad; let them ever sing for joy. Spread your protection over them, that those who love your name may rejoice in you. For surely, O Lord, you bless the righteous; you surround them with your favor as with a shield.

Psalm 5:11,12 NIV

111.

My Son, if you will receive my sayings, and treasure
my commandments within you, make your ear attentive to wisdom,
incline your heart to understanding; for if you cry for discernment,
lift your voice for understanding; if you seek her as silver,
and search for her as for hidden treasures; then you will
discern the fear of the Lord, and discover the knowledge of God.

Proverbs 2:1-5 NAS

*L*ord, I will not be deceived, for You would never harm me. For You are my heavenly Father and only that which is good and perfect comes from Your hand.

*D*on't be deceived, my dear brothers. Every good and perfect gift is from above, coming down from the Father....
James 1:16,17 NIV

113.

I will surely bless you, and I will surely multiply you.
Hebrews 6:14 NAS

114.

*L*ord, Your Word is alive and full of power. It is active, energizing, and effective. Your Word will do a powerful work in my life when I adhere to, trust in, and rely on it.

*F*or the Word that God speaks is alive and full of power [making it active, operative, energizing, and effective]....
Hebrews 4:12 AMP

...*t*he Word of God, which is effectually at work in you who believe [exercising its super-human power in those who adhere to and trust in and rely on it].
1 Thessalonians 2:13 AMP

115.

*S*o shall My word be which goes forth from My mouth;
it shall not return to Me empty, without accomplishing what I
desire, and without succeeding in the matter for which I sent it.
Isaiah 55:11 NAS

116.

*H*eavenly Father, I look to Your Word for the answer to all of life's problems. For in it contains the commands and counsels and promises You have given me through Your grace. Your Word is able to strengthen me and give me what I have inherited as a child of God.

■ ■ ■

...*A*nd I commend you to the Word of His grace
*[to the commands and counsels and promises of His
unmerited favor]. It is able to build you up and to give you
[your rightful] inheritance among all God's set-apart ones....*
Acts 20:32 AMP

117.

Come to Me, all you who are weary and burdened, and I will give you rest. Take my yoke upon you and learn from me, for I am gentle and humble in heart, and you will find rest for your souls.
Matthew 11:28,29 NIV

118.

*L*ord, thank You for sending Your Son to purchase my freedom, redeeming me from the curse of the Law. Jesus became a curse for me. Because I have received Him as my Savior the blessing that You promised Abraham now belongs to me.

*C*hrist purchased our freedom [redeeming us] from the curse (doom) of the Law [and its condemnation] by [Himself] becoming a curse for us...that through [their receiving] Christ Jesus, the blessing [promised] to Abraham might come upon the Gentiles....
Galatians 3:13,14 AMP

*I will give you a new heart and put a new spirit in you; I will remove
from you your heart of stone and give you a heart of flesh. And I will
put my Spirit in you and move you to follow my decrees and be careful
to keep my laws. ...you will be my people, and I will be your God.*
Ezekiel 36:26-28 NIV

120.

*H*eavenly Father, Your Word says that no matter how
many promises You have made, Your answer is always "Yes"
in Christ Jesus. Therefore, I respond to Your promises
by saying, "Amen, so be it in my life!"

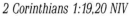

*F*or the Son of God, Jesus Christ, who was preached among you...,
was not "Yes" and "No," but in him it has always been "Yes." For no
matter how many promises God has made, they are "Yes" in Christ.
And so through him the "Amen" is spoken by us to the glory of God.
2 Corinthians 1:19,20 NIV

121.

Come, my children, listen to me; I will teach you the fear of the Lord. Whoever of you loves life and desires to see many good days, keep your tongue from evil and your lips from speaking lies. Turn from evil and do good; seek peace and pursue it.

Psalm 34:11-14 NIV

122.

*H*eavenly Father, You gave Your promises to
Abraham and to his seed. How wonderful it is to
realize, that through Christ Jesus, I am a seed of
Abraham and an heir to all that You have promised.

*N*ow to Abraham and his seed were the promises made.
And if ye be Christ's, then are ye Abraham's seed,
and heirs according to the promise.
Galatians 3:16a,29

123.

Then said the Lord to me, You have seen well, for I am alert and active, watching over My word to perform it.
Jeremiah 1:12 AMP

124.

*H*eavenly Father, I worship You for all that You have
done for me. For You have made me righteous through
Christ Jesus. You have justified me through His blood.
You have redeemed me from the penalty of sin and
You have sanctified me with Your love.

But it is from Him that you have your life in Christ Jesus,
Whom God made our Wisdom from God,...our Righteousness
...our Consecration,...and our Redemption....
1 Corinthians 1:30 AMP

To You, O Lord, I pray. Don't fail me, Lord, for I am
trusting you....your promises are my only source of hope.
Never let it be said that God failed me.
Psalm 25:1,2a; 119:114,116b TLB

*H*eavenly Father, because of Your great love for me, even when I was dead in my transgressions, You made me alive in Christ Jesus. For it is through Your grace that I am saved.

■ ■ ■

*B*ut because of his great love for us, God, who is rich in mercy, made us alive with Christ even when we were dead in transgressions – it is by grace you have been saved.
Ephesians 2:4,5 NIV

127.

This is what the Lord says – he who made you, who formed you in the womb.... "Do not be afraid...I myself will help you," declares the Lord, your Redeemer, the Holy One of Israel.
Isaiah 44:2; 41:14 NIV

128.

*L*ord, You loved me so much that You sacrificed Your only Son for me. Thank You, Father, for giving me the gift of eternal life through Jesus.

*F*or God so loved the world, that he gave his
only begotten Son, that whosoever believeth in him
should not perish, but have everlasting life.
John 3:16

129.

*I have wiped out your transgressions like a thick cloud,
and your sins like a heavy mist. Return to Me, for I have
redeemed you....And I will not remember your sins.
Isaiah 44:22; 43:25 NAS*

130.

*L*ord, I delight myself in Your Word. I meditate in it day and night. I shall be like a tree planted by the rivers of water and my life will bring forth much fruit. As I follow you, Lord, I will prosper in all that You have called me to do.

*B*lessed is the man (whose)...delight is in the law of the Lord, and on his law he meditates day and night. He is like a tree planted by streams of water, which yields its fruit in season and whose leaf does not wither. Whatever he does prospers.

Psalm 1:1-3 NIV

131.

Create in me a pure heart, O God, and renew a steadfast spirit within me. Restore to me the joy of your salvation and grant me a willing spirit, to sustain me.
Psalm 51:10,12 NIV

132.

*M*y salvation comes from You, Lord. You are my stronghold in times of trouble. You will help me and deliver me when I put my trust in You.

*T*he salvation of the righteous comes from the Lord; he is their stronghold in time of trouble. The Lord helps them and delivers them; he delivers them from the wicked and saves them, because they take refuge in him.
Psalm 37:39,40 NIV

For thus said the Lord God, the Holy One of Israel: In returning [to Me] and resting [in Me] you shall be saved; in quietness and in [trusting] confidence shall be your strength....
Isaiah 30:15 AMP

*L*ord, how comforting it is to know that no matter what problem I may face, I can approach Your throne with confidence to receive grace and mercy to help me in my time of need.

*L*et us then approach the throne of grace with confidence, so that we may receive mercy and find grace to help us in our time of need.
Hebrews 4:16 NIV

135.

*B*e well balanced (temperate, sober of mind), be vigilant
and cautious at all times; for that enemy of yours, the devil,
roams around like a lion roaring [in fierce hunger], seeking someone
to seize upon and devour. Withstand him; be firm in faith [against his
onset – rooted, established, strong, immovable, and determined]....
1 Peter 5:8,9 AMP

136.

I humble myself before You, Lord, for without You I am nothing. As I approach Your throne in prayer, I do not come on the basis of who I am or what I have done, but I come on the basis of what Jesus has done for me.

■ ■ ■

*F*or we [Christians]...who worship God in spirit...exult and glory and pride ourselves in Jesus Christ, and put no confidence or dependence [on what we are] in the flesh...].
Philippians 3:3 AMP

137.

*If you live in Me [abide vitally united to Me] and
My words remain in you and continue to live in your hearts,
ask whatever you will, and it shall be done for you.*
John 15:7 AMP

138.

$\mathcal{L}$ord, I cast my cares upon You, all my anxieties,
all my worries, all my concerns I give into Your hands. I
rest in You, heavenly Father, for I am confident that You are
watching over and perfecting everything that concerns me.

*Casting the whole of your care [all your anxieties, all your worries,
all your concerns, once and for all] on Him, for He cares for you
affectionately and cares about you watchfully.*
1 Peter 5:7 AMP

$\mathcal{T}$*he Lord will perfect that which concerns me....*
Psalm 138:8 AMP

139.

*But no weapon that is formed against you shall prosper,
and every tongue that shall rise against you in judgment you
shall show to be in the wrong. This [peace, righteousness,
security, triumph over opposition] is the heritage of the servants
of the Lord...this is the righteousness or the vindication
which they obtain from Me...says the Lord.*

Isaiah 54:17 AMP

Heavenly Father, I do not fear when bad news comes, my heart is steadfast, trusting in You. My heart is secure and I will not be afraid for You always cause me to triumph in Christ Jesus.

He will have no fear of bad news; his heart is steadfast, trusting in the Lord. His heart is secure, he will have no fear; in the end he will look in triumph on his foes.
Psalm 112:7,8 NIV

Now thanks be unto God, which always causes us to triumph in Christ....
2 Corinthians 2:14

141.

$\mathcal{L}$ord, You have given me power over all the power the enemy possesses and nothing shall in any way harm me. For greater is He that is in me than he that is in the world.

■ ■ ■

$\mathcal{B}$ehold! I have given you authority and power to trample upon serpents and scorpions, and [physical and mental strength and ability] over all the power that the enemy [possesses]; and nothing shall in any way harm you.
Luke 10:19 AMP

...$\mathcal{g}$reater is he that is in you, than he that is in the world.
1 John 4:4

142.

*L*ord, as I trust and rely upon You, I enter into
Your rest. My heart has perfect peace and I am strengthened.
For as long as I remain in that place of rest I will not
fail to receive Your perfect plan for me.

*F*or we who have believed (adhered to and trusted in and relied
on God) do enter that rest....Let us be zealous and exert ourselves
and strive diligently to enter that rest [of God...], that no one
may fall or perish by the same kind of unbelief and disobedience
[into which those in the wilderness fell].
Hebrews 4:3,11 AMP

143.

"*To me this is like the days of Noah, when I swore
that the waters of Noah would never again cover the earth.
So now I have sworn not to be angry with you, never to
rebuke you again. Though the mountains be shaken and the
hills be removed, yet my unfailing love for you will not be
shaken nor my covenant of peace be removed,*" says the Lord....
Isaiah 54:9,10 NIV

144.

*L*ord, Your grace is sufficient for me. When I am
weak, You make me strong. There is nothing that I am
unable to do when I put my trust in You. For I can do
all things through Christ Who strengthens me.

I have strength for all things in Christ Who empowers me [I am
ready for anything and equal to anything through Him Who infuses
inner strength into me; I am self-sufficient in Christ's sufficiency].
Philippians 4:13 AMP

145.

*H*eavenly Father, You have promised that no weapon formed against me shall prosper. For when the enemy comes at me like a flood, You will raise up a standard against him.

*W*hen the enemy shall come in like a flood, the Spirit of the Lord shall lift up a standard against him.
Isaiah 59:19b

146.

*H*eavenly Father, through faith in Your Word, I walk in victory. I am an overcomer in every situation. For You have made me more than a conqueror through Christ Jesus.

■ ■ ■

*F*or everyone born of God overcomes the world. This is the victory that has overcome the world, even our faith.

1 John 5:4 NIV

*...W*e are more than conquerors through him who loved us.

Romans 8:37 NIV

147.

*J*esus said...
*I have told you these things, so that in Me you may have [perfect]
peace and confidence. In the world you have tribulation and trials
and distress and frustration; but be of good cheer [take courage; be
confident, certain, undaunted]! For I have overcome the world. [I have
deprived it of power to harm you and have conquered it for you.]*
John 16:33 AMP

148.

*H*eavenly Father, I will not be afraid. For You have
not given me a spirit of fear, but a spirit of power,
and of love, and a sound mind. I will lay down and
sleep in peace, Lord, for You cause me to dwell in safety.

*F*or God hath not given us the spirit of fear;
but of power, and of love, and a sound mind.
2 Timothy 1:7

I will lie down and sleep in peace, for you alone,
O Lord, make me dwell in safety.
Psalm 4:8 NIV

149.

*H*eavenly Father, You have clearly proven Your love for me by the fact that while I was still a sinner Christ died in my place. I have been justified through the blood of Jesus and I am no longer under Your wrath, I am under Your grace.

*B*ut God demonstrates his own love for us in this:
While we were still sinners, Christ died for us. Since we
have been justified by his blood, how much more shall
we be saved from God's wrath through him!
Romans 5:8,9 NIV

150.

*L*ord, You are my refuge and my fortress. I put my
trust in You. I rest secure in Your promise of protection.
For You have commanded Your angels to surround
and guard me in all my ways.

■ ■ ■

*I*f you make the Most High your dwelling – even the Lord,
who is my refuge – then no harm will befall you, no disaster
will come near your tent. For he will command his angels
concerning you to guard you in all your ways.
Psalm 91:9-11 NIV

151.

*Put on the full armor of God so that you can take your stand
against the devil's schemes. For our struggle is not against flesh
and blood, but against the rulers, against the authorities,
against the powers of this dark world and against the spiritual forces
of evil in the heavenly realms. Therefore put on the full armor of God....
Stand firm...take up the shield of faith, with which you can extinguish
all the flaming arrows of the evil one. Take the helmet of salvation
and the sword of the Spirit, which is the word of God.*
Ephesians 6:11-17 NIV

152.

*H*eavenly Father, Your Word lives and abides
in my heart. I have confidence in You, Lord, for You
have promised that if I ask for anything according to
Your Word, You will always hear and answer my prayer.

*T*his is the confidence we have in approaching God:
that if we ask anything according to his will, he hears us.
And if we know that he hears us – whatever we ask –
we know that we have what we asked of him.
1 John 5:14, 15 NIV

153.

*H*eavenly Father, You have given me everything
I need to live a life of victory. You have given me
great and precious promises so that I might partake
of Your nature and walk in abundant life.

*His divine power has given us everything we need for
life and godliness through our knowledge of him...he has
given us his very great and precious promises, so that through
them you may participate in the divine nature....*
2 Peter 1:3,4 NIV

154.

When I choose to obey Your Word, Lord, You promise
to fill my life with Your blessings. All these blessings will
come into my life when I choose to walk in Your ways:
I will be blessed in the city and blessed in the country.
My children will be blessed.
My food will be blessed.
I will be blessed when I come in and blessed when I go out.
My enemies will be defeated before me.

155.

You will command Your blessings upon my home
and everything I put my hand to will prosper.
Everyone will see that I am blessed of the Lord.
You will give me abundant prosperity in every area of my life.
You will bless the work of my hand.
I will lend and I will not have to borrow.
I will be the head and not the tail.
I will be a success and not a failure.
For You are my heavenly Father and You have promised it.
Deuteronomy 28:2-13
(author's paraphrase)

References

Connie Witter has been a Christian since she was 6 years old. She believes that developing a strong personal relationship with God through studying His Word and prayer are essential to living a victorious Christian life. Connie has taught home Bible studies and is the author of a Bible study entitled *Inheriting the Promises of God*. In it she teaches how she received victory in her own life through putting her absolute trust in the promises of God's Word.

Connie is married to a wonderful husband, Tony, and is the mother of three beautiful children —Justin, Jared, and Kristen. They make their home in Broken Arrow, Oklahoma.

To contact the author, write:

Connie Witter
P.O. Box 3064
Broken Arrow, OK 74013-3064

Additional copies of this book
are available from your local bookstore.

HARRISON HOUSE
Tulsa, Oklahoma 74153

The Harrison House Vision

Proclaiming the truth and the power
Of the Gospel of Jesus Christ
With excellence;

Challenging Christians to
Live victoriously,
Grow spiritually,
Know God intimately.